Love
Energy

Changing the World One Soul at a Time!

Amber Leanne Martin

BALBOA
PRESS

A DIVISION OF HAY HOUSE

Balboa Press books may be ordered through booksellers or by contacting:

Balboa Press
A Division of Hay House
1663 Liberty Drive
Bloomington, IN 47403
www.balboapress.com
1 (877) 407-4847

Because of the dynamic nature of the Internet, any web addresses or links contained in this book may have changed since publication and may no longer be valid. The views expressed in this work are solely those of the author and do not necessarily reflect the views of the publisher, and the publisher hereby disclaims any responsibility for them.

The author of this book does not dispense medical advice or prescribe the use of any technique as a form of treatment for physical, emotional, or medical problems without the advice of a physician, either directly or indirectly. The intent of the author is only to offer information of a general nature to help you in your quest for emotional and spiritual well-being. In the event you use any of the information in this book for yourself, which is your constitutional right, the author and the publisher assume no responsibility for your actions.

Any people depicted in stock imagery provided by Thinkstock are models, and such images are being used for illustrative purposes only. Certain stock imagery © Thinkstock.

Print information available on the last page.

ISBN: 978-1-5043-3175-3 (sc)
ISBN: 978-1-5043-3176-0 (e)

Balboa Press rev. date: 05/20/2015

Love - An intense feeling of deep affection.

Energy - Is often seen as a continuum
that unites body and mind.

My goal is to attract as many people as possible to question everything they have ever known about their world around them. I aim to instill a new way of living deep into their beings, while removing animosity moving towards the future!

Contents

Spiritual Girl

My eyes are wide open because
It was the day my time had come
I was ready to be woken up
Feeling different from everyone

It was like starting all over again
This time clear and fully supported
In myself I had found a friend
My vision of life no longer distorted

This was my brand new way
That I can look at this world
In this way I will always stay
Because I am a spiritual girl

I know that deep inside
Farther than I've ever looked
My soul jumped on for the ride
And every chance there was I took

Looking at the real way of life
Different from what I saw before
For me my choices are always right
This blew open all of my doors

My life connection has deepened
Staying open I have always tried
Not just from bed time sleeping
I am AWAKE my soul finally alive

Love Energy

If we fill our world with love
And love when love is not around
It will lift your soul high above
Levitating you off the ground

Love rushing through your veins
Trust what you are feeling
It now doesn't feel the same
Because you are believing

Love shining guiding you to grow
See the light that fills your soul
Taking you where you need to go
Through darker days that take their toll

There is magic deep inside of you
And there is energy seen so rarely
I know it will always come through
When love is seen this clearly

Oneness can be our rebirth
Love can teach us to be better
This is what carries the entire earth
And love is what brings us all together

Colors of the skies

The colors of the skies
Or the fields full of fire flies
Sunny days I have in the rain
My life will never be the same

Birds chirping as they fly
Flying I would love to try
Soaring through the wind so high
Who knows what I might find

But I love water most it seems
It is the bases of our beings
Middle of the ocean on a boat I dream
Floating on the waves writing poetry

The stars each with deeper meaning
Their shine bright and incredibly beaming
I know it will always be all right
I know this when the moon shines bright

Trees are so ancient strong and so tall
With shades of green that covers them all
Stop and listen to the sound of their call
They burst out with colors come the fall

The first snow fall in winter
And watching everything shimmer
White beautiful and untouched
I just love this sight oh so much

We can go through all of the seasons
Overlooking simplicity for many reasons
Caught up in nothing but distractions
It is time to reevaluate some of life's fractions

Dreaming

As I close my eyes
And lay my head down
Finally I no longer
See or feel the frown

I think about all
That my life could be
Then to my surprise
It is there for me

As I am dreaming
Everything that I am
It makes life worth living
Not someone else's plan

The thoughts all around me
My vision is so clear
All I have been wanting
It's all just right here

Going through my head
Like wind through the rain
While I am dreaming
I no longer feel the pain

The tasks that I have
Ones I must complete
Before I get to this dream
I must begin to seek

When I am always out searching
At times I feel there's no landing
I am one person
So I try to be understanding

So if dreaming will take me
To where I want to be
Then I will close my eyes
And I will dream

Treasures

Take the time to learn about
All life's resonating things
Find the treasures you believe
That your unique life should bring

One day when you completely
Know how to open up your mind
Discoveries of what's always been there
The ones you could never find

Do not wait until too late
For it's your time to shine
You must have the faith that you can be
Achieving your life on time

Shine

Be kind and you may find
Relax rewind it will ease your mind
Rewind be kind
You just may find yourself this time

Do good and good will come as it should
Do right and right won't be far out of sight
Do good and do right
Feel great you just might

Fall in love and love will help you rise above
Be the beauty and beauty will
shine through you truly
Feel the love and see the beauty
This combination will let you roam freely

Love

When you can share
And when you hug
When you can care
Is when you love

If you stay strong
If you rise above
Admitting when you're wrong
Is when you love

Always be nice
And always be kind
When you love
It will ease your mind

Taking care of others
And taking care of you
Is when you love
And treat yourself too

Keep a smile
And good energy
Stay positive
To keep your love upbeat

Surrounded by nature
And surrounded by fun
Surrounded by ones who care
Is filling you with love

So never stop loving
Everything and everyone
Be the best that you can be
And love will set you free

Me

I am what I am
To see what I see
I know only I
Can understand me

To be by myself
I feel so alive
But when I am not
I sometimes hide

I grew up thinking
That life was so wonderful
But when I got older
I also got told

If I ever had one chance
To turn back time
To know then what I know now
That chance would be mine

I could change my mistakes
And make them all better
But if I did that I wouldn't have learned
From one's I made when I was younger

Struggle

I know what it feels like to struggle
So hard trying just to get by
In those moments we are far from humble
Holding it all in to not break and cry

First you find yourself down in rock bottom
Trying to get back to the top again
Everything becomes so sour and rotten
Impossible for the broken pieces to mend

Once you are down there
And your thread about to break
Something comes out of nowhere
Revealing your ultimate fate

Something inside will keep you going
Stay strong enough to pull through
Soon you will come out of this growing
And become rewarded for all that you can do

Unknown

I'm working to get my soul out clean
Stopping me just don't even bother
Constantly feeling I'm swimming upstream
Charting through these unknown waters

I had to want my life to go another way
Even sometimes when it was a lot of work
Struggling to carry myself to another day
My purpose for life in the shadows it lurked

If I deeply connected to my emotions
I learn they come from down in my soul
And if I can really trust my intuition
My gut tells me first what I need to know

Some days it takes all I have inside of me
But those are the days I know I must try
Finally free to be reaching my dreams
Now to my old life I must say goodbye

I am following a more thought out plan
That I may not understand or see done
But I got my feet planted and took a stand
Risking everything for new found freedom

The Past

Most of us still remain in the past
Bad memories we cannot escape
We choose to let the negative last
Instead of just being in the present day

We all have our different stories
Of why it was so terribly sad
So many have troubles and worries
Because our past was just so bad

What good does it ever do for you
If you keep living in what is gone
Just do all that you really want to
Rid what always has gone so wrong

I chose to do this when my timing was right
Not holding on helped me figure it out
I knew I was free to see with new sight
Letting go was simple I had no doubt

It does not matter how hard you try
There's nothing that can change it
Before your life passes you by
You should try letting go a little bit

Life is the moment you live in now
Not memories created long ago
Not all of us understand how
To forget what we already know

You can always change your reality
And see new things you once had lacked
Putting your past behind you sets you free
If you would just stop holding yourself back

Now you must go out there and get them
And you'll see it's just a matter of time
Nobody can take your freedom
When you say it is rightfully mine

Each Day

You must go through the bad
Before you get to the great
You can overcome feeling sad
When happiness you appreciate

Don't block yourself off
From having the life that you crave
It's time to be your own boss
Find it inside of yourself to be brave

It's never too late no matter your age
To be the best person you can be
Be sure not to feed into your rage
No need to express with intensity

You must overcome the obstacle
That is purposely in your way
For you to become unstoppable
Getting stronger each day

Growing

This life only comes around once
When everything is new
From the day you open up your eyes
It's all about discovering you

Thoughts and dreams
Are building as you grow
Experiences are what you make
But excitement is what you know

The Light the dark colors or not
We create things to our expense
Planned or not it's what we have thought
Come to find life is way more intense

Things are a figment of our imagination
We are all something of someone else's creation
As it reaches through you to your foundation
Tapping into all of your sensations

So what you make life to be
All of us so different but one
It's something truly real for you and me
No one knows what life will become

Whatever it takes

Open for your deepest dreams to flow
You must do whatever it will take
To get to where you want to go
Don't you fear what is at stake

You will have some major highs
Also the deep dark lows
But if you can soar through the sky
Life will reveal where your path goes

Patience will always be the key
Staying humble will bring you ahead
Have the desire to uncover your destiny
So you can live your dreams instead

Inspiration you will no longer lack
Find it in yourself to follow through
Stop listening to what holds you back
These words I write meant just for you

Do not give up along your way
You can always handle what arises
Every beginning comes with a brand new day
No dream is to far no matter what the size is

So go do what you're always thinking of
Those dreams you have pushed to the side
But you must live them with meaning and love
And most importantly you must make the time

So no more excuse after excuse
Start believing your dreams will manifest
A new way will be introduced
And the Universe takes care of the rest

I will always go after my dreams
To the best of my abilities
Most don't understand it seems
That they too can have all of these things

Process

It's a process you must take
And won't happen overnight
Believe that it is your fate
Even when it's far out of sight

Do not let your fear sink in
As hard as it may try
This is your time to begin
Before opportunity passes by

It will lead you to new places
You have only seen in your dreams
And show you some new faces
Who show you what this means

You must remain persistent
When finding who you are
Be open, not resistant
Of your life you're the star

It is your creativity
That is the purpose of your life
Explore to the best of your ability
To fly higher than a kite

Journey

This has been an incredible journey
Not long ago embarked upon
Nothing is left not one little worry
Finally my life doesn't seem wrong

I've searched for more meaning
The answers hitting me strong
My path I can now see clearly
With a sense of feeling I belong

I just want you to see what I see
This process is real can you trust it
All that you have to do is believe
And the Universe will conspire every bit

Starting to find what I'm looking for
This is my chance all over again
When opportunity starts to soar
I will bring you with me my friend

Magic

This magic is real
Not always seen with the eyes
It is something we can feel
From deep down inside

In all that is around
Start to become a believer
Listen to the whispering sound
To tune your inner achiever

Reach for the stars
In all the mystical ways
Your dreams won't be far
If you cherish your days

Do not question it why
To trust the natural flow
Hop on for the magical ride
And you too will naturally grow

We always say maybe tomorrow
How about next month or next year
The steps are there for you to follow
But only you can get yourself here

Intuition

Do you know what it means
Or where it is coming from
Guiding you through your dreams
You and your higher self as one

This is something you must follow
As you make your decisions
At first it may be hard to swallow
When trusting your new visions

Coming to you out of the blue
Always moving you toward
Showing you the steps to do
To keep you going forward

Never will it lead you astray
When calling out for help
Things will start to go your way
Your path already paved out

All our lives we've had these powers
To help in any given situation
When used as your signal routers
It becomes the gift of intuition

Law of Attraction

The Law of Attraction
Is the power of the mind
Ask believe receive
What you seek you shall find

Look far inside of yourself
What does the heart desire
Ask the whole of the Universe
In order to start the fire

Believe with every part of you
That what you want is already yours
Believe every day for it to be true
So you too can open up new doors

Receive all of your desires
With a wide open heart
Deep gratitude takes you higher
Being great is doing your part

With good positive thoughts
Manifest your dreams and all of the perks
Remember to ask believe receive
And that is how the Law of Attraction works

Gratitude

The meaning of gratitude
Is to truly be grateful
Have a positive attitude
And never be hateful

Be thankful that you're on your path
And be thankful for all that you receive
Be thankful for everything you already have
And be thankful for all that you believe

Never want something so bad
That you're not grateful for all that you have
Try to remain happy not sad
Focus on making yourself laugh

Always show love
For absolutely everything in your life
If you always show love
Then it will always be alright

Treat with kindness and love
Your family and your friends
For they will always be there
When your heart needs to mend

So you see the way of life is just this
Be kind loving and thankful
For a life full of incredible bliss
And always remember to be grateful

Chakras

Remember these colors
They are not like the others
These ones are special
Connecting you to a higher level

Let's start with the root red in color
This is your foundation there is no other
Located at the base of your spine
Keeping you grounded within time

Now for abundance move up to your sacral
You will find this located just below your navel
This is your sexual sense taken in all seriousness
Orange provides the ability to
accept any new experiences

Yellow the color of our Solar Plexus
This helping find our confidence within us
In your stomach boosting your self-esteem high
Open this up and you will be in control of your life

Here is a special one its color green
Overflowing love like you've never seen
Center of the chest just above the heart
There is no question this is where to start

Now this is your throat and this is your truth
Our ability to communicate color light blue
Keep this passage way clear for
things to get through
When your throat is blocked you
are not expressing you

Center of your forehead, still blue
but a few shades dark
This is the trigger what will ignite the spark
Our imagination intuition and
wisdom grows thicker
Creating our ability to focus on
and see the big picture

Now for our connection to our higher selves
It's a beautiful purple and something incredibly felt
The crown of your head fully connected and in bliss
Align yourself and you'll find you are pure divineness

Get in tune with your body and its reason for things
You just may uncover your unique divine wings

Change

Can you magnify
Your third eye
Please just try
To say goodbye

The dragonflies
Good little spies
In the skies
They signify

Changing lives
Can you visualize
Dreams in disguise
Emotionalize

With them empathize
Time to rise
Above your size
It's finalized

Yoga

Yoga can be fun
But not for everyone
When getting yoga done
You become one

Finding your Zen
Believe everybody can
Let your body bend
And your life will mend

Lifting your spirits
With new eyes see it
You consciously submit
When in silence you sit

Going inside oneself
This is how you find yourself
Removing all of your self-doubt
Is what yoga's all about

Meditate

It is what makes you radiate
Through the things that you do
It helps you not to contemplate
The things you have to choose

It helps you to appreciate
The stillness without concern
This supports you to concentrate
And discover what you want to learn

It helps you not to complicate
The process of your thoughts
With the om vibration aspirate
To untangle all of your knots

Promise yourself to set a date
If you want to be balanced and stable
This is the path that uncovers your fate
But all your cards must come to the table

This finds silence to get your soul awake
It will always help to fill the holes
Doing this daily makes you feel great
And for yourself you can create new roles

There cannot be any better bate
To see what is inside of your soul
Start today it is never too late
To find the you nobody else knows

Helping you quickly to find your pace
And guidance will shine the light
It works with you to speed up the rate
Believing in you makes everything right

You will always find peace this way
Letting your soul come through
Honoring the divine within Namaste
Honoring me and honoring you

Signs

Notice your signs
Look with your eyes
No need to stare
They are everywhere

You can look up and down
Signs exist all around
You can seek far and wide
Let them be your guide

What is meant just for you
Will resonate through
Something then will spark
Removing your dark

But trust in your instincts
The thing that links
Your mind and the soul
To the signs of your road

If you can stop debating
Life will stop hesitating
Coming at the perfect time
Have you been asking for a sign

Answered Prayers

They come in different ways
Not what is expected by you
Answered prayers come everyday
Showing you what to do

Don't look at losing things you own
Because it opens space for the new
These things your soul has out grown
And this is only growing you

Just pray for your desires
Or when you need some guidance
Only then it all conspires
And it all starts to make sense

However you must have patience now
Because it can take some time
Never ask the Universe how
And it will always turn out fine

Your prayers will always be heard
But not all are given to you
Asking for everything is a little absurd
With this process you must be true

Be sure of what it is you need
And put emotion behind your prayer
You must start with planting the seed
And go completely with it from there

Illuminate

Be kind to yourself
And smile from within
Speak gently to yourself
And let the loving begin

Let that illuminating light
Deep inside of you
Shine so bright
It is what's true

Take care of your body
In healthy ways
Eat healthy and naturally
Every single day

Dress yourself nicely
And groom yourself up
It will make you all smiley
It will make you light up

Try to stay positive
And try to stay happy
Do all you can to give
And always be laughing

These are the daily things
That you must do
Making yourself happy
Is taking care of you

Chemical Garden

I feel so happy eating this
It makes me feel so strong
Fruits and veggies in all its bliss
Have now gone chemically wrong

The ability of the mind and body
Is greater than it seems
The healing is truly godly
When eating earthly protein's

The power of plants all around
Is nature's healing medicine
Anything that comes from the ground
There's really no comparison

Awareness

Gmo's have got to go
Most around the world they know
It is killing us and not so slow
They say yes when we say no

Pay attention to what's being sold
I know the truth will be told
That even when this food is old
You won't find a trace of mold

They continue to print false labels
While we believe in their fables
Mass produced for everyone's tables
Eventually our health disables

We must not be careless
Or this will be endless
In complete fairness
All we do is bring awareness

Healing yourself

Look for the cause
Instead of the cure
Put your knowledge on pause
We can heal I'm sure

This way seems so crazy
Not done in ancient past
It makes us all so lazy
And we must change this fast

Every one of us can heal
Embracing new things
So incredibly real
What this energy brings

Find your own way
To be completely natural
And just one ordinary day
You become healed after all

Helping the world

We must all do our part
To reach out in some way
Search deep in your heart
When beginning each day

You can find your passion
Something you truly love
Anything to make it happen
Finally able to rise above

Why not get others involved
It's easy to get them excited
I know problems can be solved
When you and I are enlightened

Shining through as magnificent
It can be anything you want to do
Helping the animals the environment
Or the people less fortunate than you

You could volunteer your time
Or donate things you no longer use
Anything that's in your creative mind
You should always put it to good use

Never give up when things are rough
To help the world be a better place
I understand trying times can be tough
But I know this is something we can face

We are all here for one another
With each and every single day
So be loving and kind to all others
A guarantee to send the bad away

Complete

Helping you
Is helping me
And others to
Set them free

The ones who seek
To change their path
There I'll be
And I'll be fast

I can provide
Things to question
Let fear subside
This is my suggestion

Helping you
Is good for me
It's what we do
To be complete

Children

If you get down to their level
You will begin to learn
That if you are very careful
Everyone gets their turn

Talk it out in a calm way
So they actually understand
If you remember this everyday
You become a parent and a friend

You will gain the respect
When you can explain
Have your children reflect
Instead of complain

I know it is tough
And stressful at times
When the going gets rough
The energy combines

Not always easy
But just learn as you go
Not always pleasing
When the parents say no

Stick to your structure
You're doing it right
Do not let them puncture
Your rules overnight

No need to give in
When repeatedly asked
For everyone a win
When given their tasks

Show them love not to lack
Without knowing that you did
With every rule left intact
You're teaching every kid

Children are incredibly smart
So loving and very kind
Learning to them a talented art
Inside their beautiful mind

Believing

I was at the cutest kid's party
We helped to save a bumble bee
She had just turned four
And he was turning three

Struggling in a pool of water
We watched as he tried to get out
All of a sudden I had realized
That helping him we cared about

So I grabbed a toy shovel
And the kids stood close to watch
The bee did all he could to climb on
I felt his pain more than I had thought

We laid him down on the side
Giving him his space to breathe
I wasn't sure he would survive.
But every kid there had believed

So we picked the bee some dandelions
And we saved a life that day
Regaining strength as he ate
Then got up and flew away

Living beings

All living beings
Have the natural ability
They know what this means
Working in synchronicity

Birds fly forever
No matter the weather
With beautiful feathers
Split second decisions together

Grazing the lands
Are my animal friends
Reach out our hands
Because their work never ends

Swimming the seas
Underwater life in the reefs
And every one of them believes
That working together frees

So many are out there
And intricate with care
Paying attention is rare
Creatures are every where

We all have our reasons
For what we believe in
No matter the seasons
And what we are thinking

We can learn from them
And from our fellow man
If together we ran
Changing this earth we can

Animals

What would you do
If you were in their shoes
Which way would you turn
And what would you choose

I will bring truth to the forefront
Because all animals are my friend
Not one life more important
Each and every one I defend

The depths of their souls
And the sadness in their eyes
Some not more than hours old
Some in cages all of their lives

When did we as a society say
Hey your mine to control
Say goodbye forever to the light of day
Let's build an empire were on a roll

We will crucially use and abuse
Until this planet is officially wiped out
Well I stand up and I refuse
Because they all deserve to be cared about

Authority

Do not let them make you feel so small
When they over power you acting so tall
It will not matter to them at all
Lurking in the shadows hoping you'll fall

Out to make every person crawl
Done at our own will it's our own call
You may as well bang heads off the wall
Until we make changes once and for all

Why with our power we always must stall
Walking and running this never ending hall
You mustn't forget to be the perfect doll
Because everyone's hiding at this mascaraed ball

Don't you see how much were enthralled
Everyone dreams of a luxurious sprawl
The time has come to make the big haul
And everyone out there we need you all

Behind the mask

Can't all of you out there truly just see
That we absolutely do not need money
Why not make this world for free
Is it really that hard to believe

This system is designed to keep us in place
And we blindly follow at their irrational pace
Keeping us ignorant and dumb just in case
We don't rebel and blow up in their face

Why would they do this to us you ask
Because they want us fulfilling
every one of their tasks
These elitists' hidden behind their masks
When overpowered their systems will crash

We must find a way to erase all of this madness
And once we start it will happen so fast
Let's put an end to all of the sadness
Learning from the mistakes made in the past

We say it's ok for them to tell us what to do
They physically and mentally destroy us too
Secretly doing things they are hiding from you
Seeping into your skin just like a tattoo

Really stop and think about all of these things
Working for the man what does it bring
Waking up each morning when the alarm rings
Do not be late when that work bell dings

This isn't our purpose and not real at all
To be this obedient when the higher up calls
So be the one who partakes in the fall
Of this evil presence so peace can stand tall

Were subjects to media truth they don't feed
They work for the major corporations that lead
Loving were sick over weight and in need
Watch your tv but don't you dare read

Literally suffocating us so we can't breathe
Filling us with cancers and other dis ease
Haven't you noticed them clear cutting trees
In the future will our air be free

Killing off the life we have in our seas
Break out the pesticides to take out the bees
Such brutal acts of cruelty to other living beings
Not wanting to inflict pain
makes us crazy it seems

They are way too close to having

their mission complete

Laughing at all of us down on our knees

Why don't they want people to be free

Make time for work over your families

We all just want happiness and out of this please

These puppet masters controlling our destiny

Now let's make the truth your reality

Because living this way is killing you and me

United we stand divided we fall

People come forth
And together well stand
We will fight for you all
We will fight for this land

If we choose to go against
Our sisters and our brothers
The energy becomes intense
No love for one another

How can we live in a free world
If we try and conquer each other
Think about every scared boy or girl
How about their father and mother

We do not ever stop to think
The consequence our actions produce
Feel the karmic energy on the brink
It is important that these issues reduce

Think about the things you can do
To be a part of changing what is wrong
But first it must start with inside of you
Finding yourself and where you belong

Echo

Hello everyone here is my plea

This message is for all of you to see

Are you out there living in your zone

Or are you out there feeling completely alone

What is happening all over the world

Changes for every boy and girl

Happening is a massive awakening

Do you even know what this all means

Bring love into consciousness

To achieve truly divine happiness

Care about your sisters and brothers

Without them there'd be no others

Spread around some acts of kindness

I think it would help clean up some of the mess

Don't be a prisoner in your own blindness

Life is all about showing your kindness

Peace on earth is what we all desire

But our egos too high to put out the fire

We have created a fictional reality

False illusions most fail to see

Caught up in a man-made society

Never letting Mother Nature to be free

Can't you see we are lost in a trap

We won't move forward while still looking back

These controlling bullies now wanting to frack

It's time to take over it's time they are sacked

We must accept changes and all new things

The song of life will help us sing

Don't be afraid and don't be shy

We must freely live our lives

But were still not alone no just look up to the sky

You'll see they have been with us all of our lives

Can you tell me what to you is inspiring

And what if you followed your dreams

Could you believe in the things you cannot see

Trusting in yourself to just let it be

If you let your soul shine through
And let what is inside out of you
Be creative and go get inspired
Follow your passions to live what you've desired
You are who you are so be who you want to be
Following your instincts will set you free
Do not underestimate the words that I speak
Begin your self-discovery and new eyes you will seek
Be a part of this worldwide transformation
It is all so simple if we choose
to remove complication
Don't let fear hold on to you any longer
Search for your confidence it
always makes us stronger
We are all connected to one another
So please don't separate yourself from others
Everything that surrounds us with which we are one
Nature living beings the moon and the sun
Look within only yourself

Figure it out what you're all about

Work on issues and remove your self-doubt

Wake up to the reality we have to get out

If we say enough is enough

Then we must stop acting so tough

All this time we have fought

Now time we take back what cannot be bought

When the world of the people

See it as just that simple

We put aside our differences

And begin new experiences

No possessions no financial burdens

Live this way and everybody wins

We must start with who we are

just look into the mirror

Then you will begin to see yourself clearer

Only you can make yourself complete

And living this way can be so concrete

If you stop and look you will see

This world will heal if we let it be

Take part in the action the time is now

Do what makes you happiest don't worry about how

We are the changes we wish to see

So get up off your butt and onto your feet

Do not pass this off for generations to come

This is our home responsibility for everyone

Yes I know there is bad out there

But the bad helps us see who really cares

Why must we let some live in despair

Tell me do you think this is fair

It is our natural right to be equal

But we all have been divided apart

It is time now create our own sequel

And it will begin straight from the heart

Dedication

Through the times when I just didn't understand my life purpose and what was meant for me to do, I had two very special people in my life who took initiative to help guide me down my path. If it wasn't for both of you being so helpful and patient with me, I don't know where I would be today. I could not be more happy or proud to dedicate my first book to you both! You have been my inspiration throughout this whole process and always kept believing in me.

Thank you
Nick Jasper
&
Reilly Marie Martin

You & Me

You came into my life the exact
moment I needed you
Not knowing our connection
was different from before
Over time passing your heart showed pure and true
And you have lifted my soul to
a place where it can soar

Inspiration from your heart and
you only ever mean well
I know our deepest desires will always come true
Because you have made me believe in myself
As much as I always believed in you

More dreams to uncover as this journey continues
Something only you and I will ever understand
Everything turns out so right just being with you
So I'll always be there to reach for your hand

Now I can move throughout this world fearlessly
You showed you will always have my back
The universe has sent its protection over me
This undying love you give keeps life in tact

Reilly

The little girl full of light
She is my girl Reilly
Her love brightens up the night
And her energy so lively

Reilly is so warm and kind
Her spirit is so free
Without her in my life I find
That I just would not be me

It's all gone by so very fast
No longer baby Reilly
The days with you have been a blast
My much cherished memory

Reilly words cannot express
How proud I am of you
And every day you impress
With all that you can do

My love today is the day
Intelligent little Reilly
You are finally turning eight
And of you I think so highly

Love is oneness
Oneness is everything
Everything is love- ALM